Part 1

14 Animals in the Quran

Activity & Coloring Book

By Halimah Bashir
Art by Laila Ramadhani

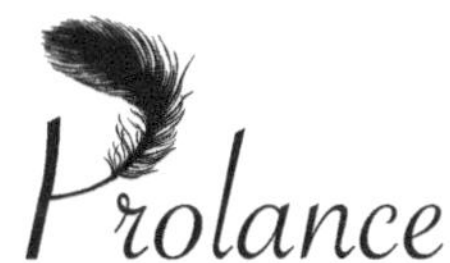

California, USA
www.prolancewriting.com
© 2024 Halimah Bashir
ISBN: 979-8-9899703-7-7
All rights reserved. No part of the publication may be reproduced in any form without prior permission from the publisher.

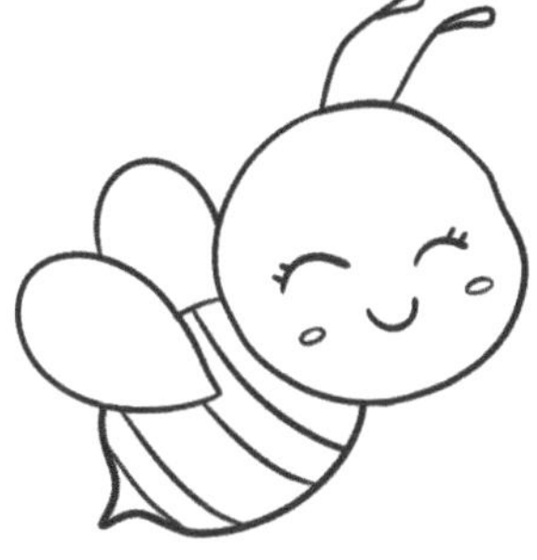

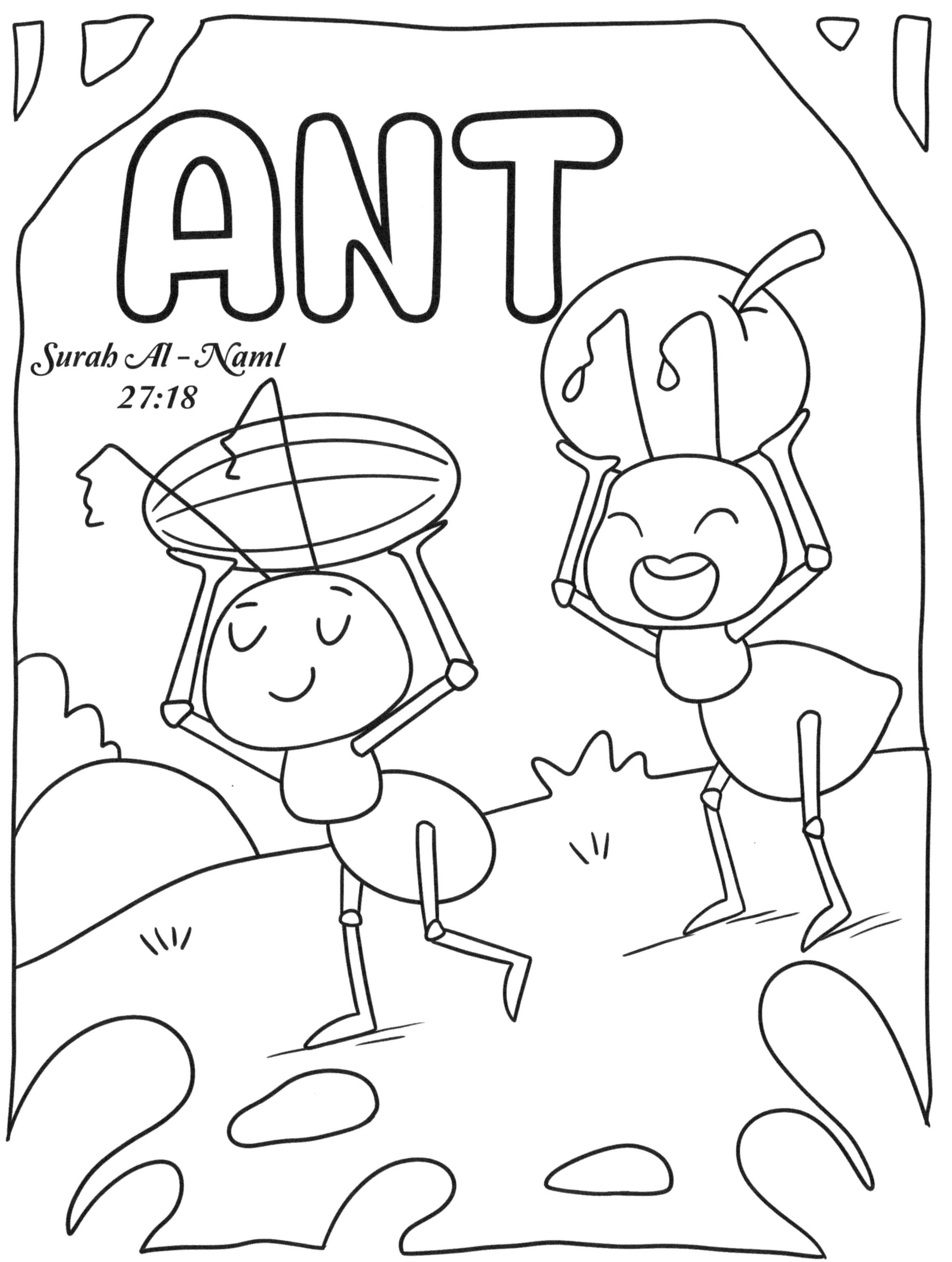
ANT
Surah Al - Naml
27:18

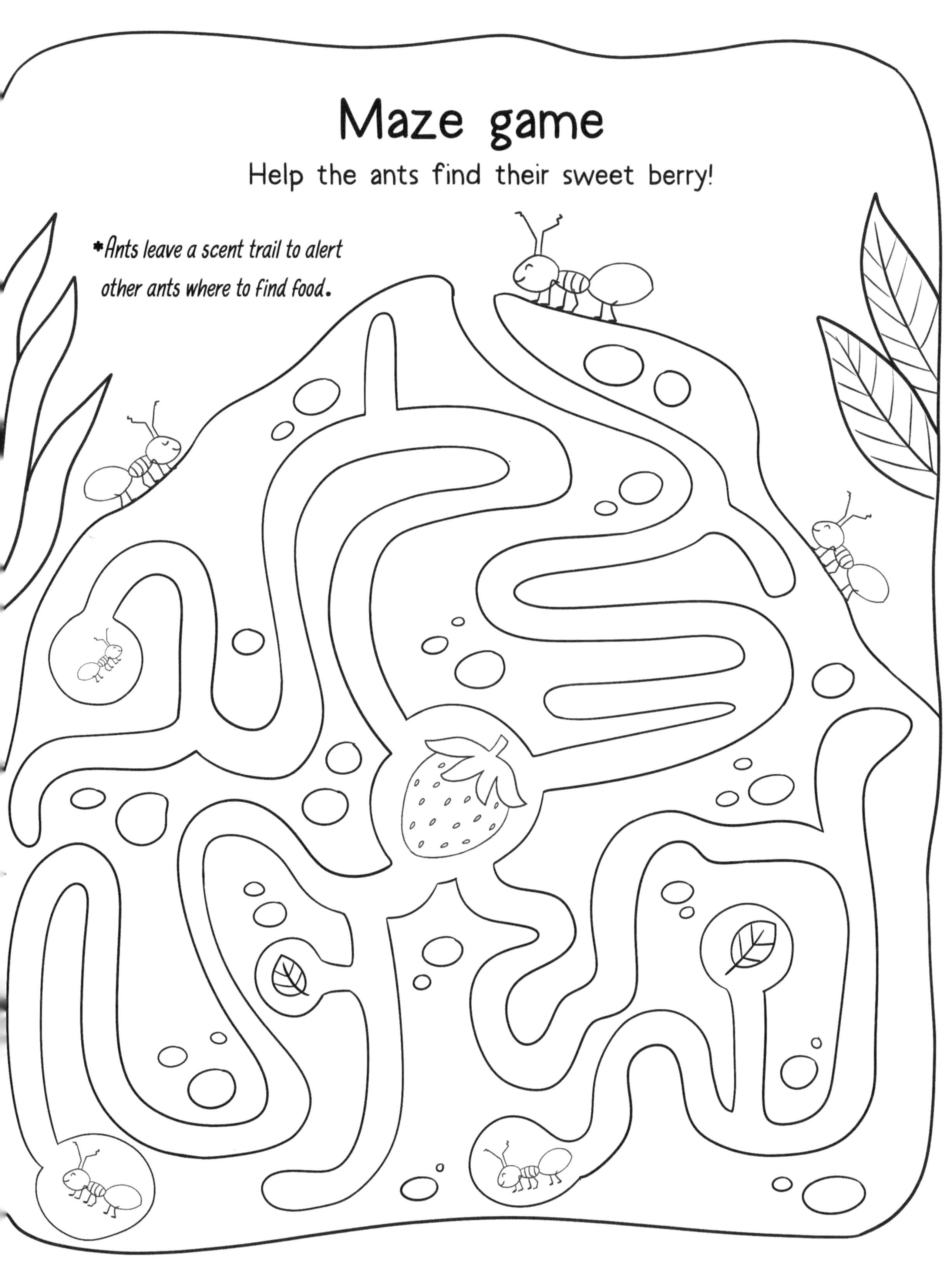
Maze game
Help the ants find their sweet berry!
*Ants leave a scent trail to alert other ants where to find food.

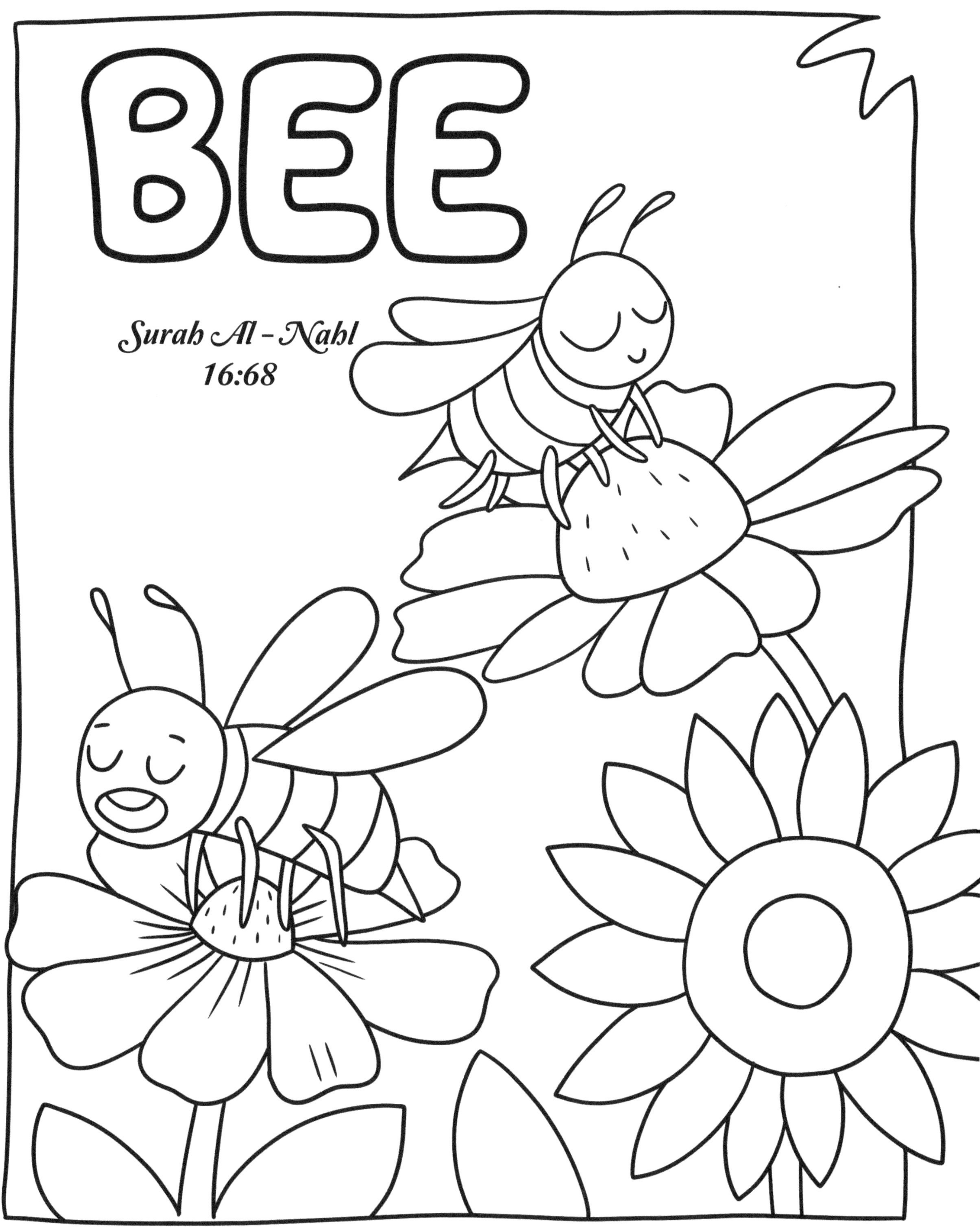
BEE
Surah Al - Nahl
16:68

Shadow matching

*A bees brain is as small as a sesame seed.

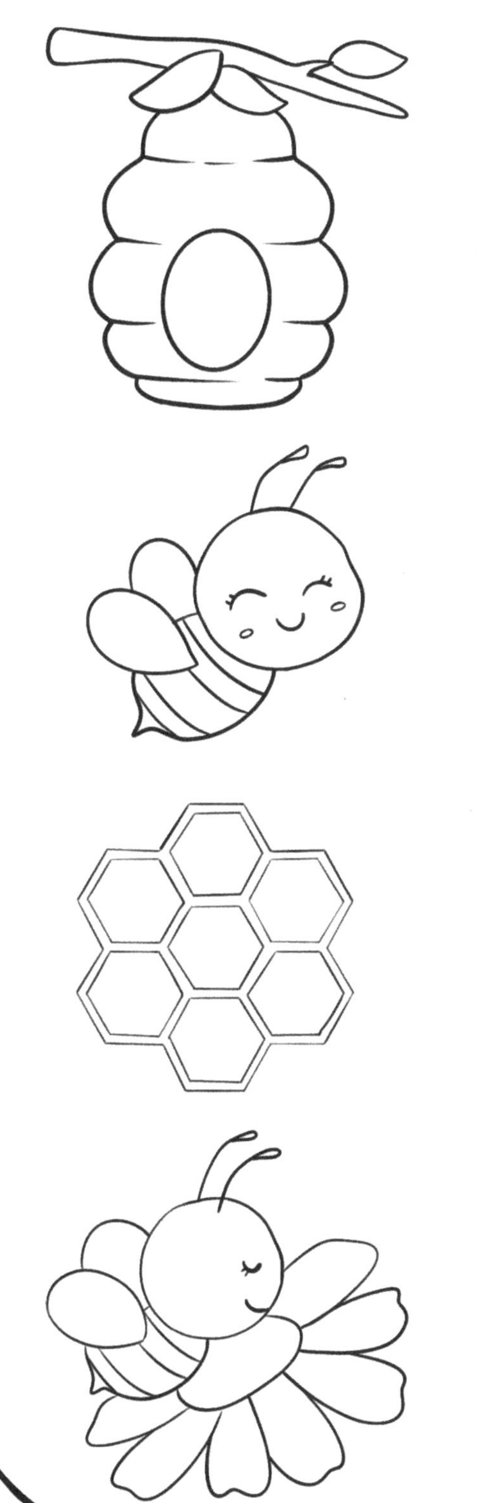

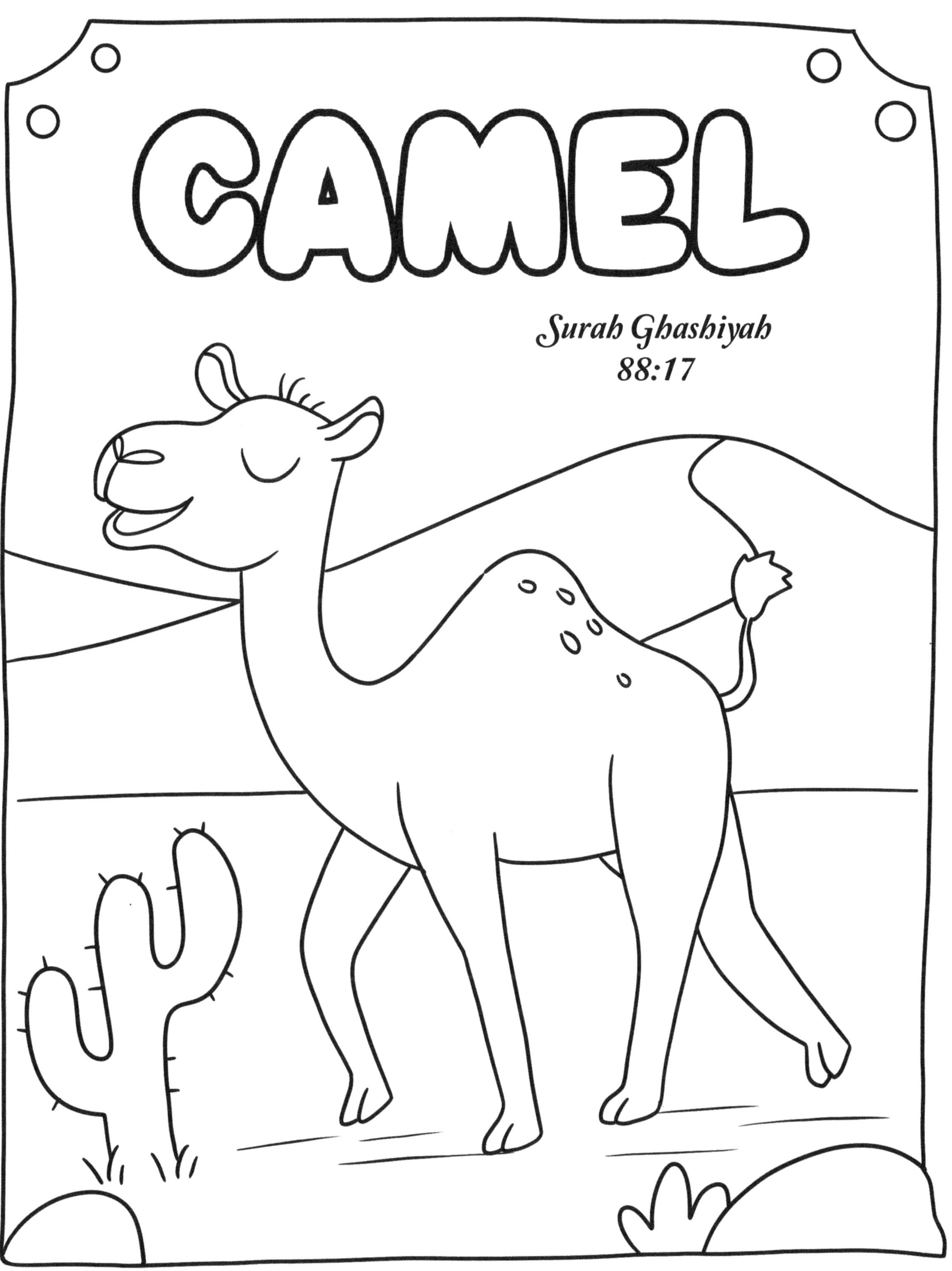
CAMEL
Surah Ghashiyah
88:17

How to draw a camel

* *The Prophet's camel was named Qaswa.*

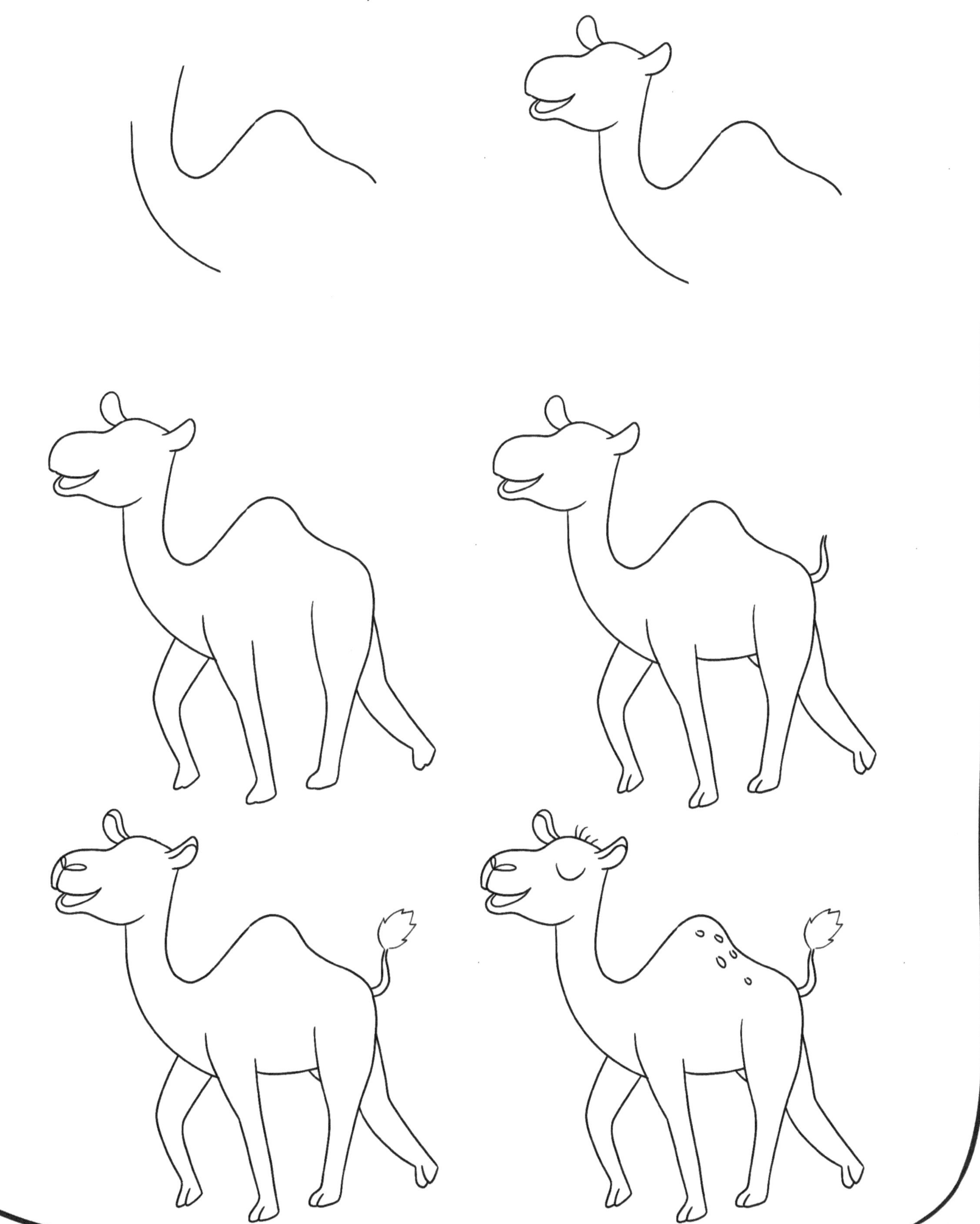

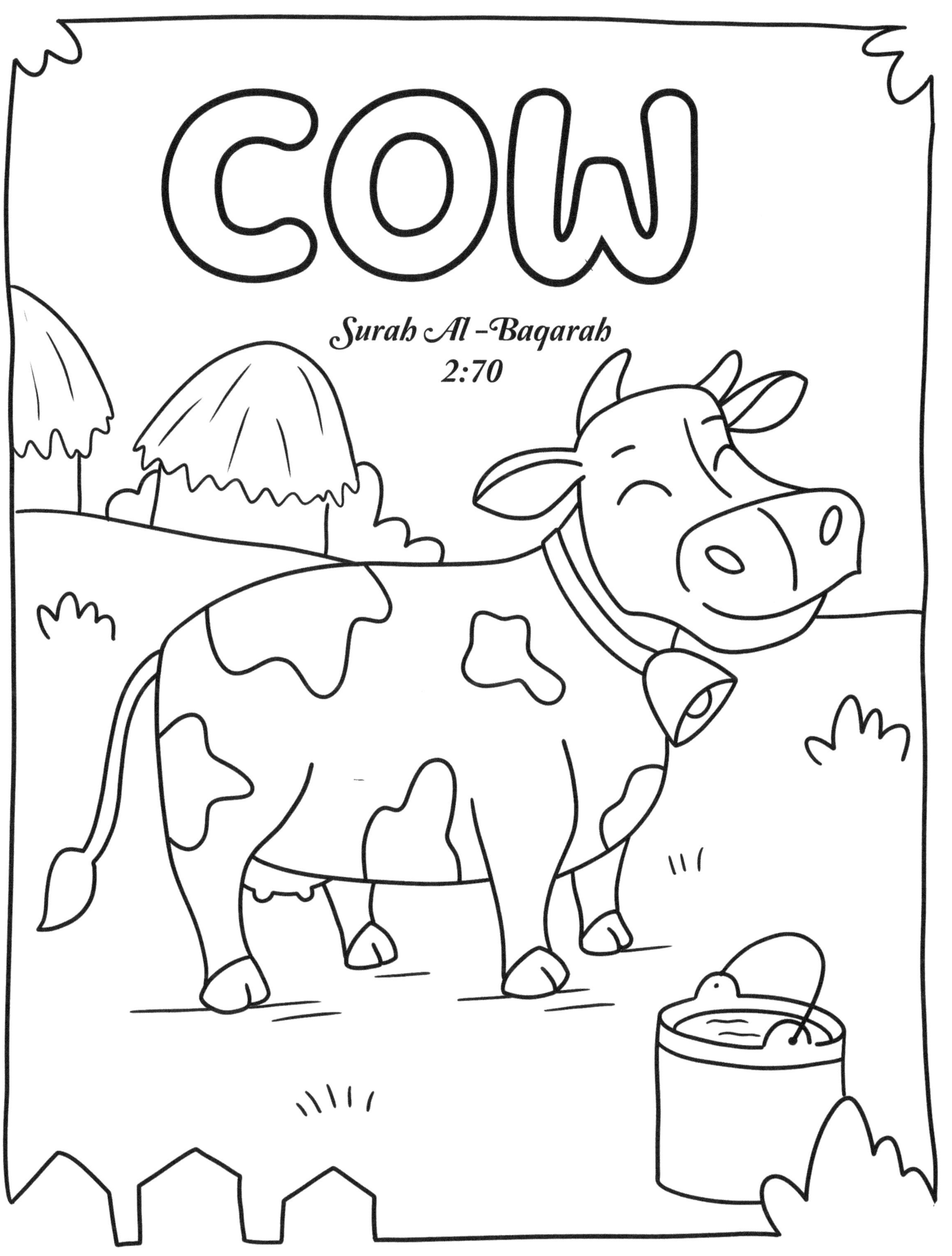
COW
Surah Al -Baqarah
2:70

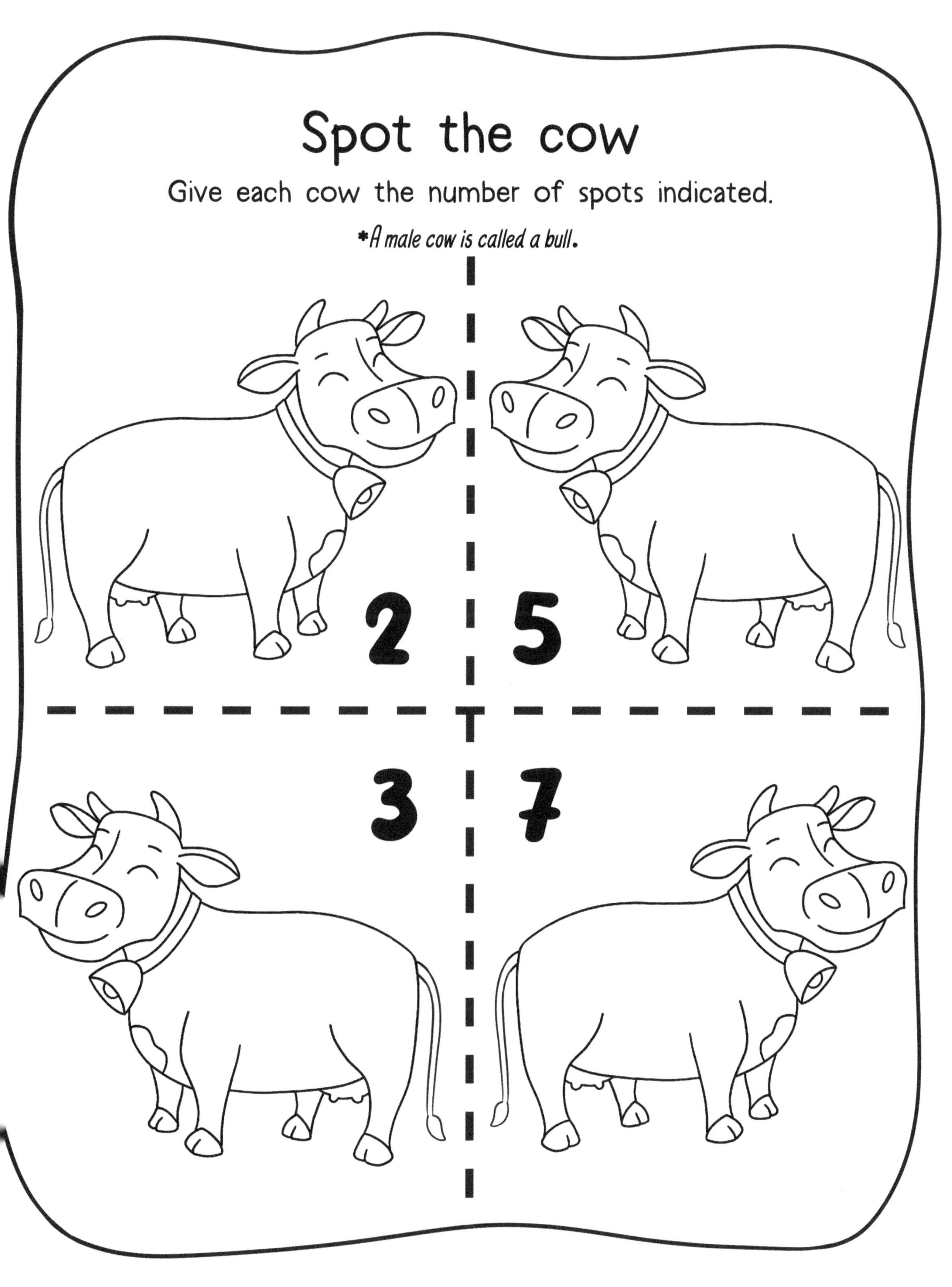
Spot the cow
Give each cow the number of spots indicated.
*A male cow is called a bull.
2
5
3
7

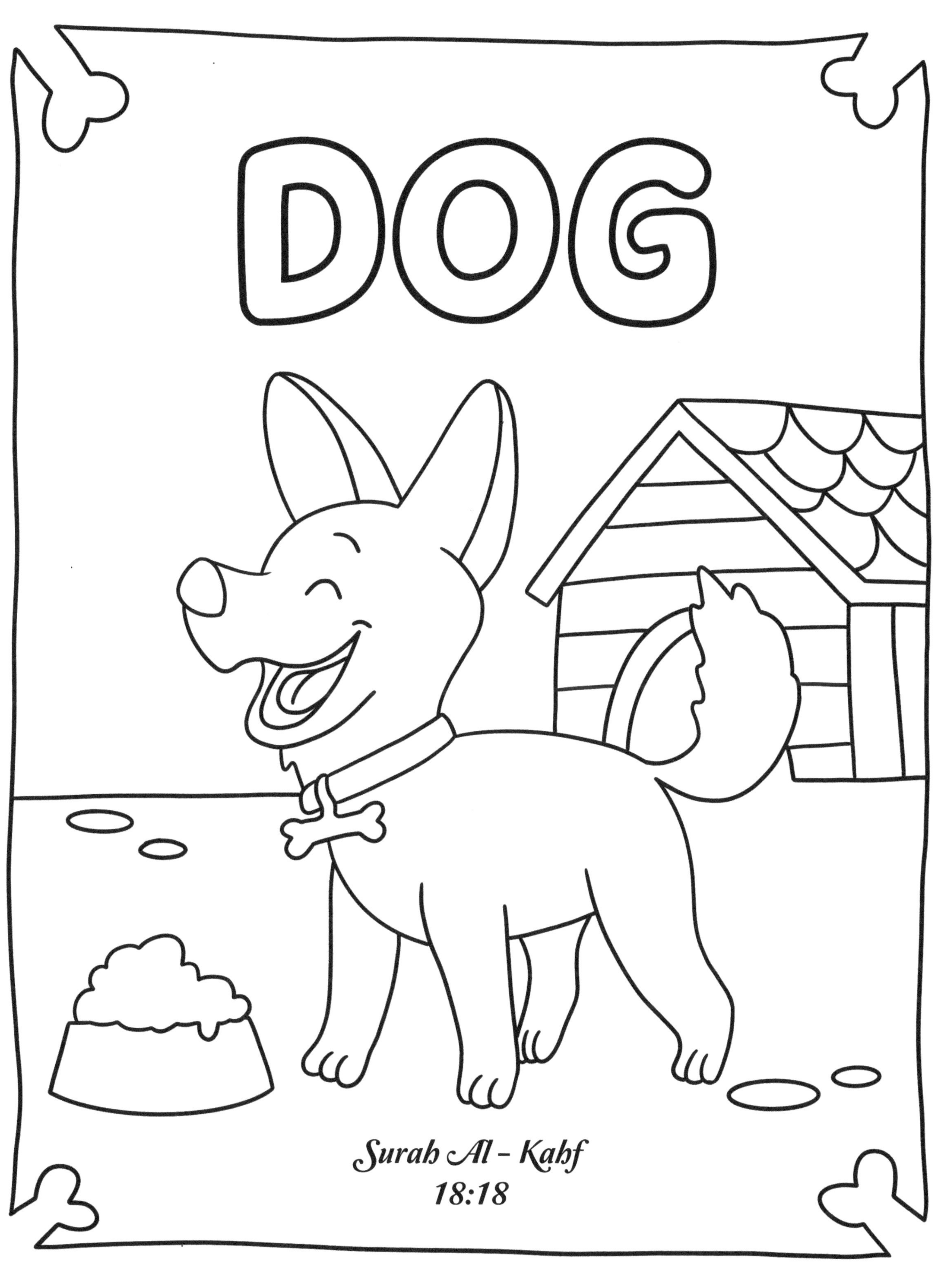
DOG
Surah Al - Kahf
18:18

Same size dogs

Find the two dogs in each row that are the same size.
Color them.

**Puppies are blind and deaf when they are born.*

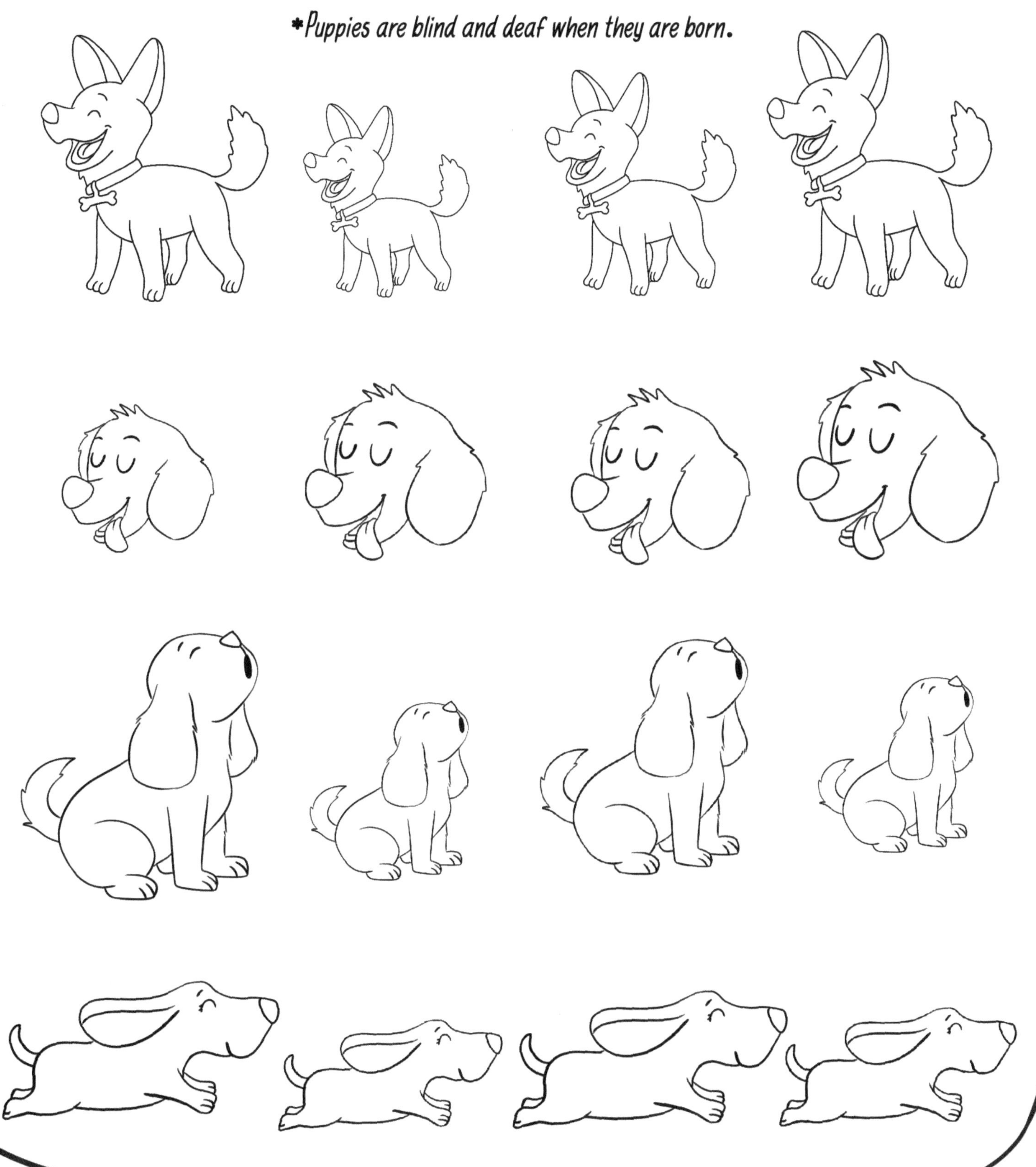

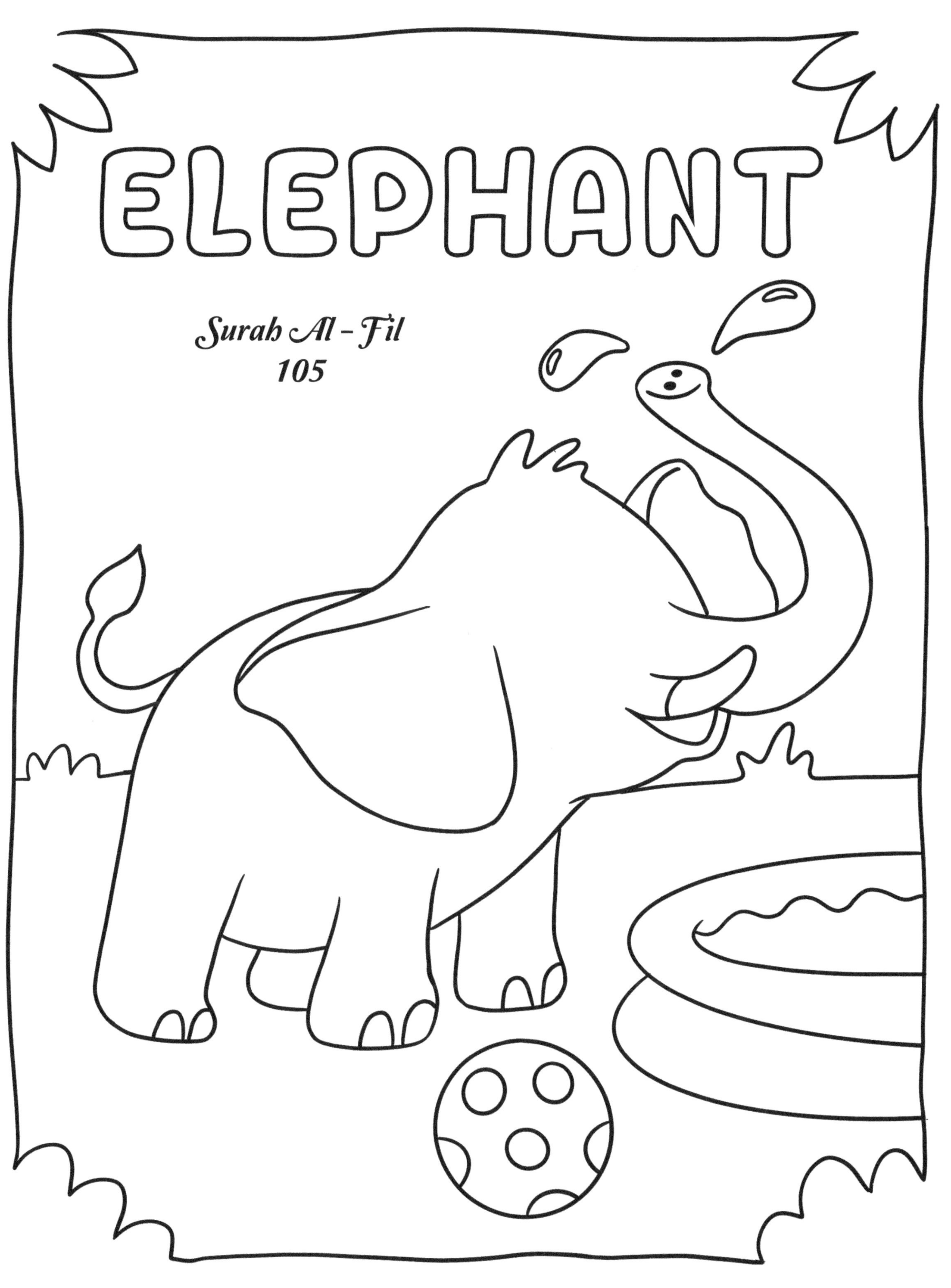
ELEPHANT
Surah Al - Fil
105

Connect the dots

**Elephants are very intelligent animals with amazing memory.*

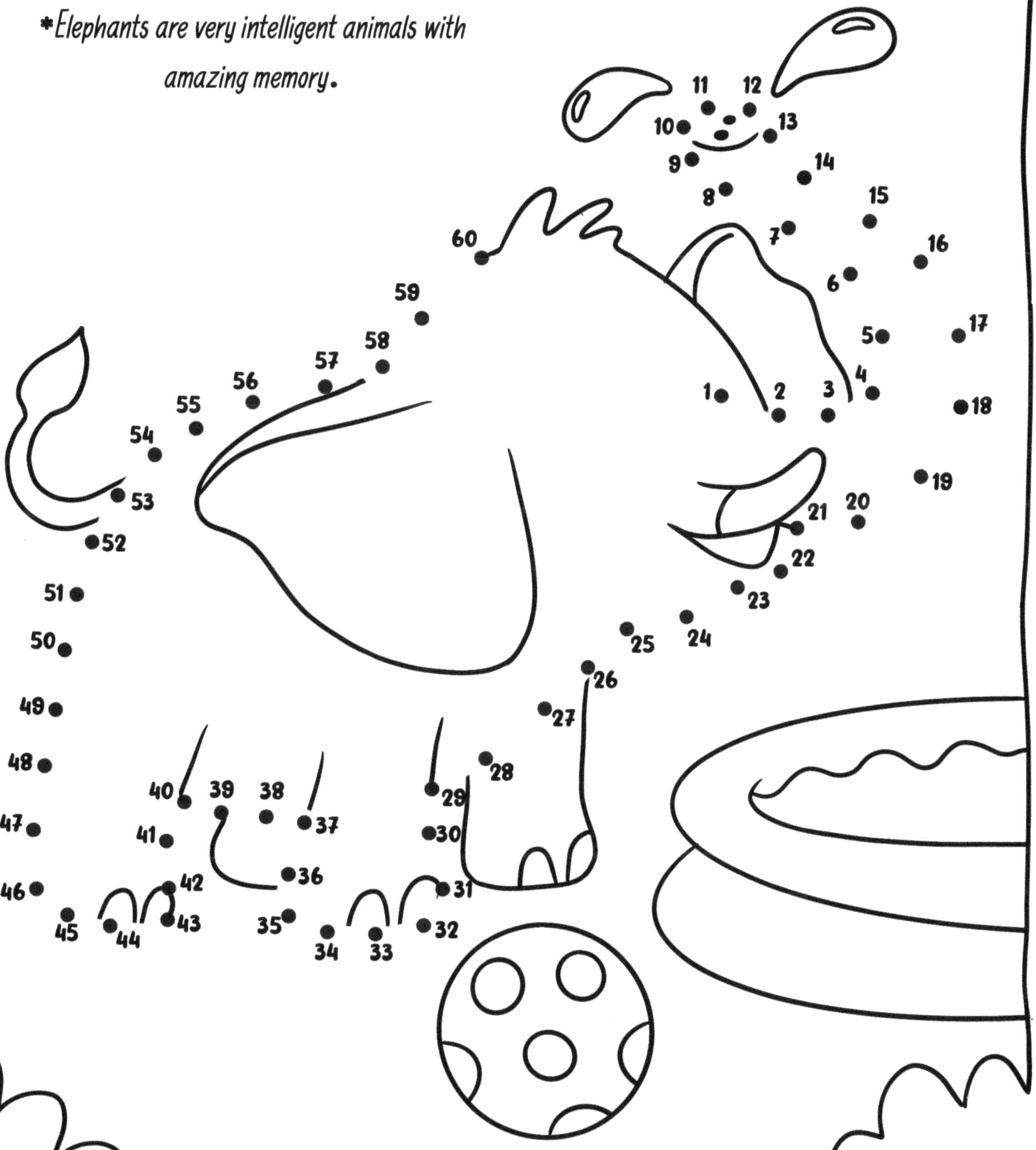

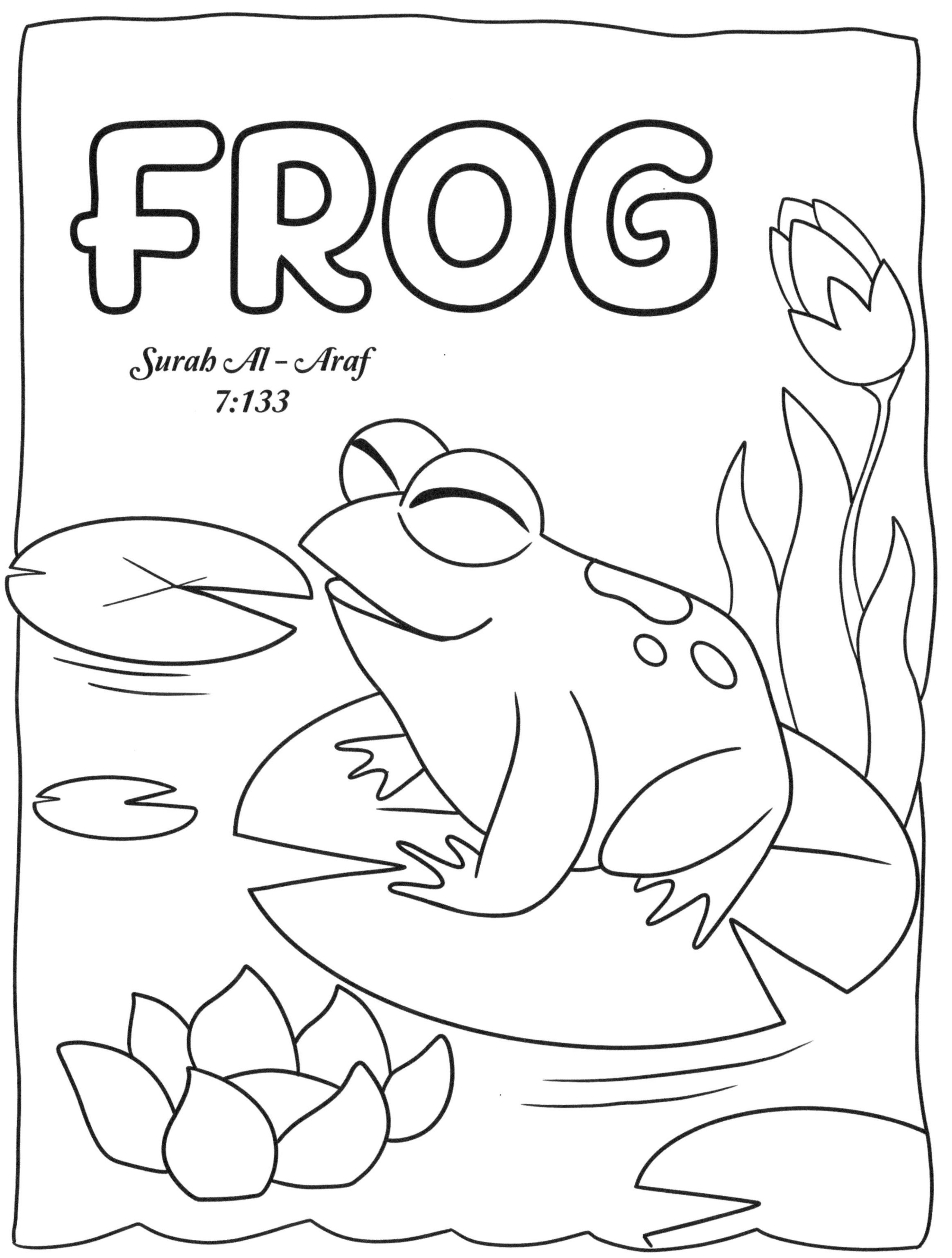
FROG
Surah Al - Araf
7:133

Color the frog

and all the foods that frogs eat.

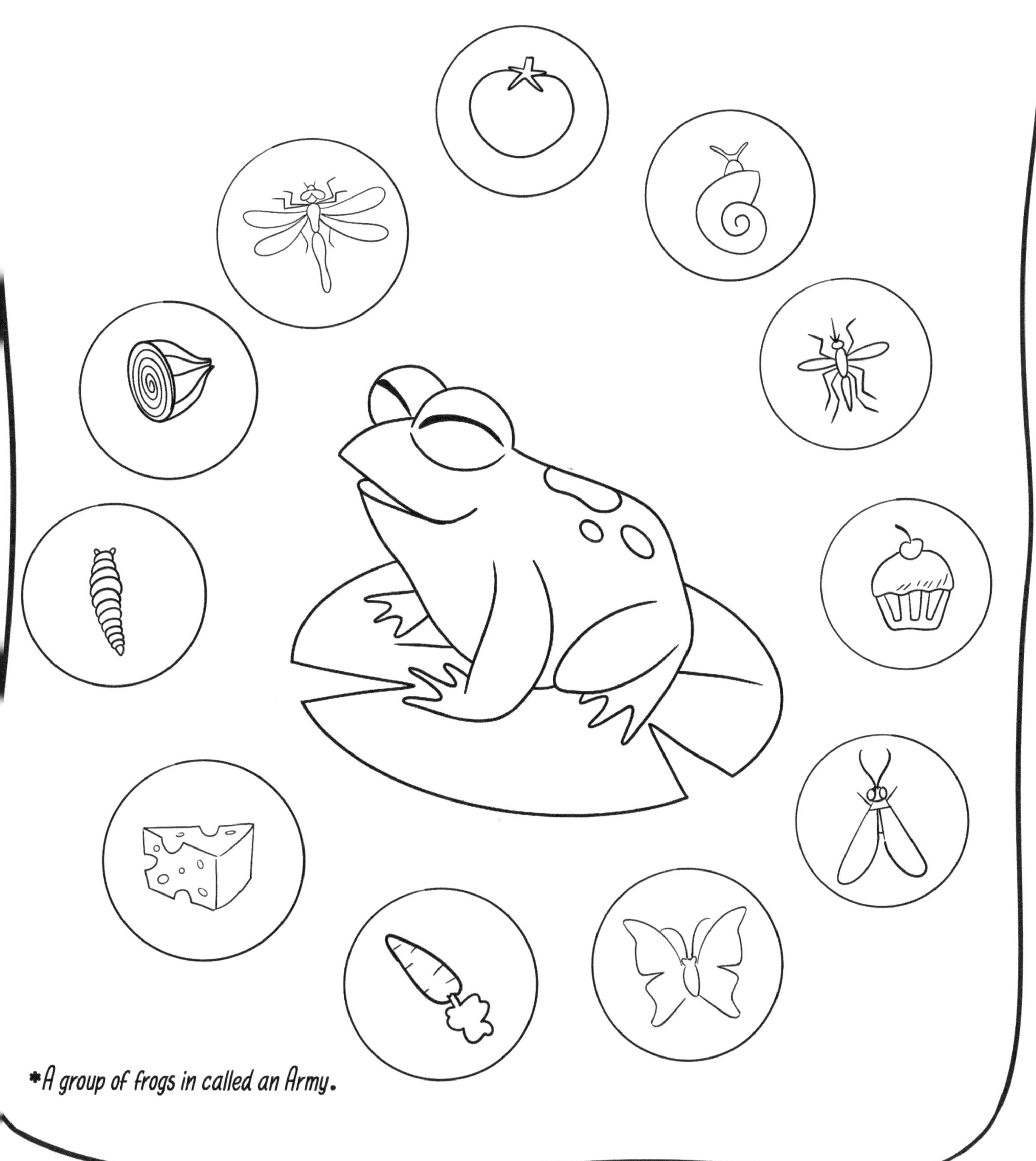

*A group of frogs in called an Army.

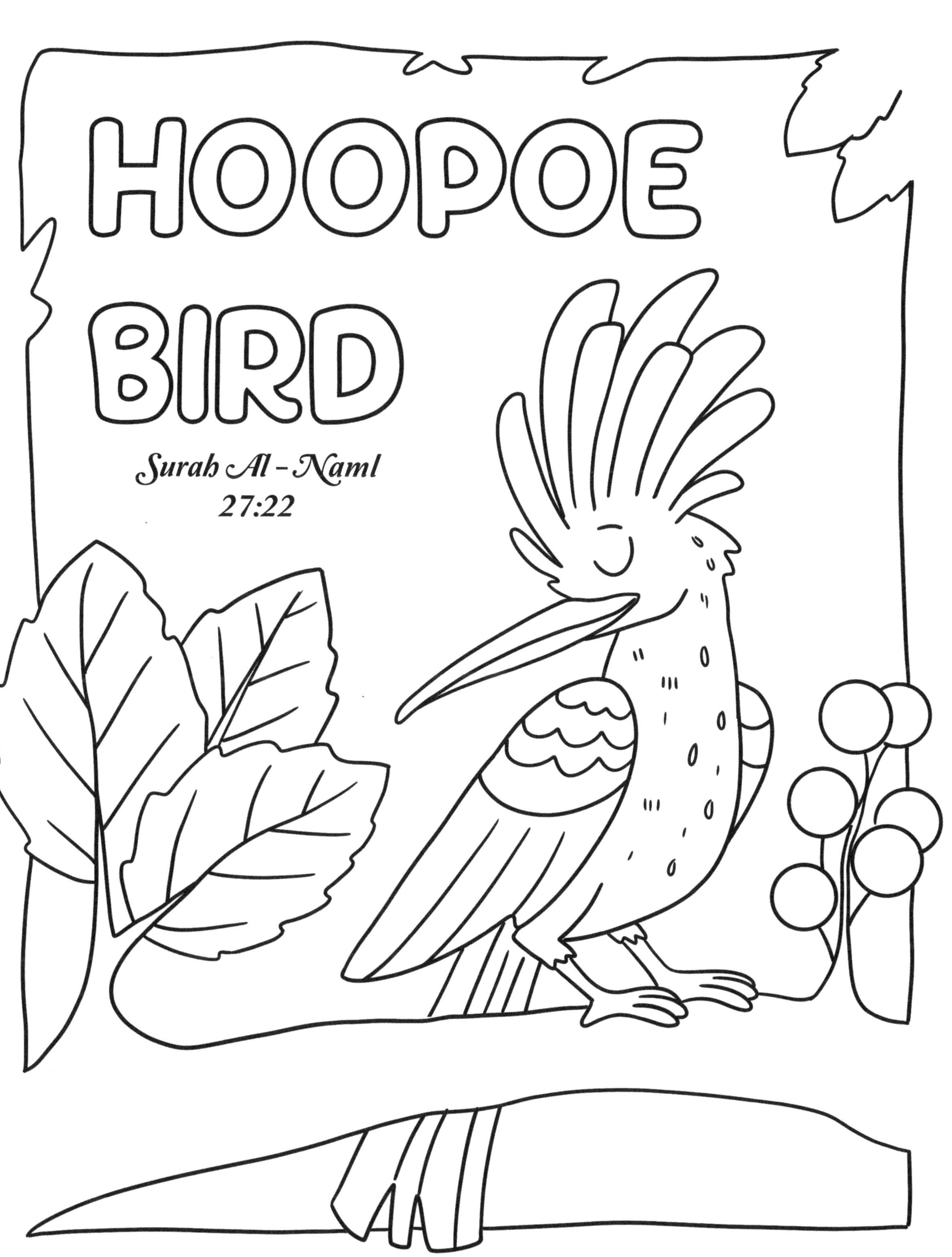
HOOPOE
BIRD
Surah Al - Naml
27:22

How to draw a hoopoe bird

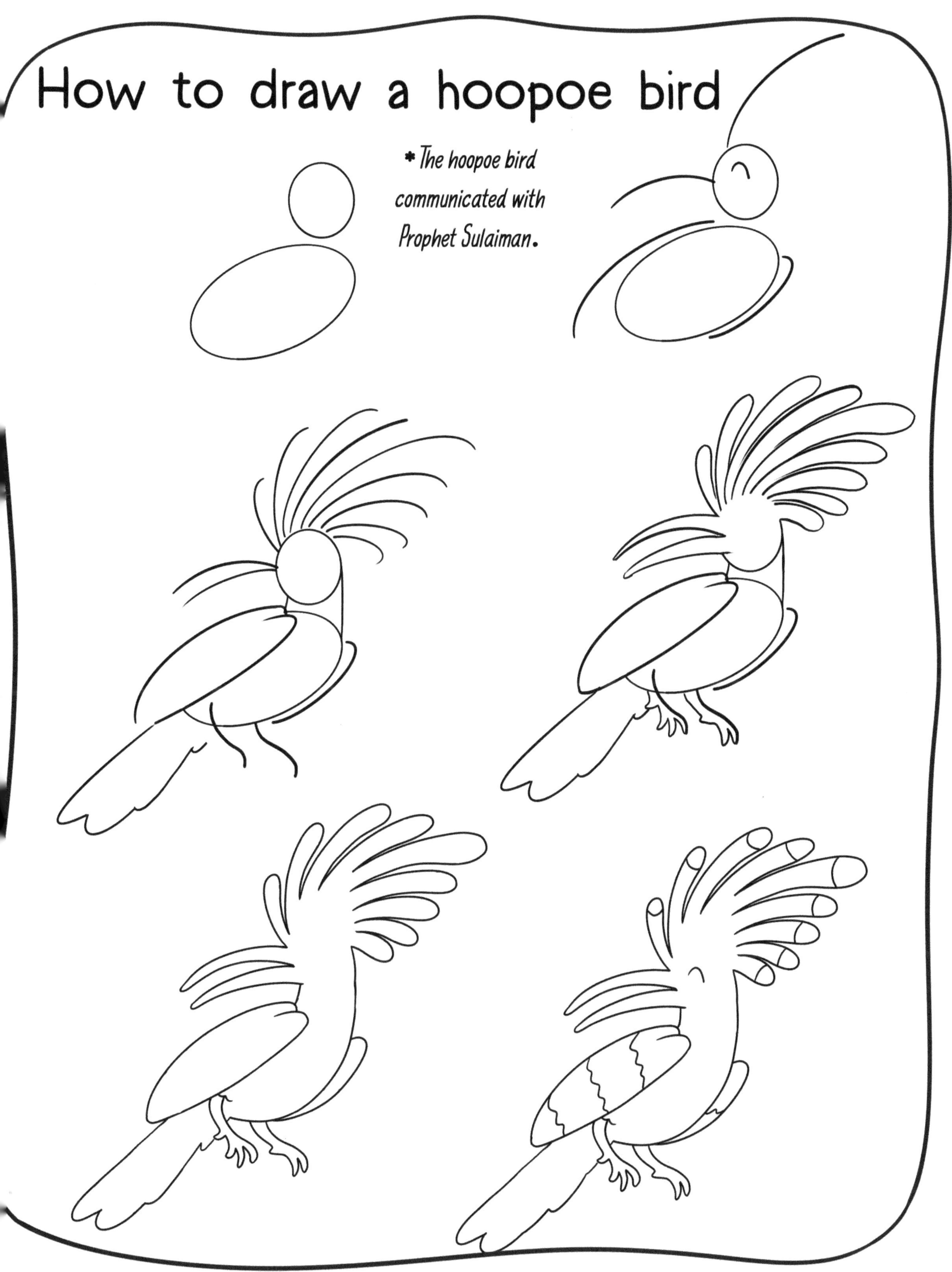

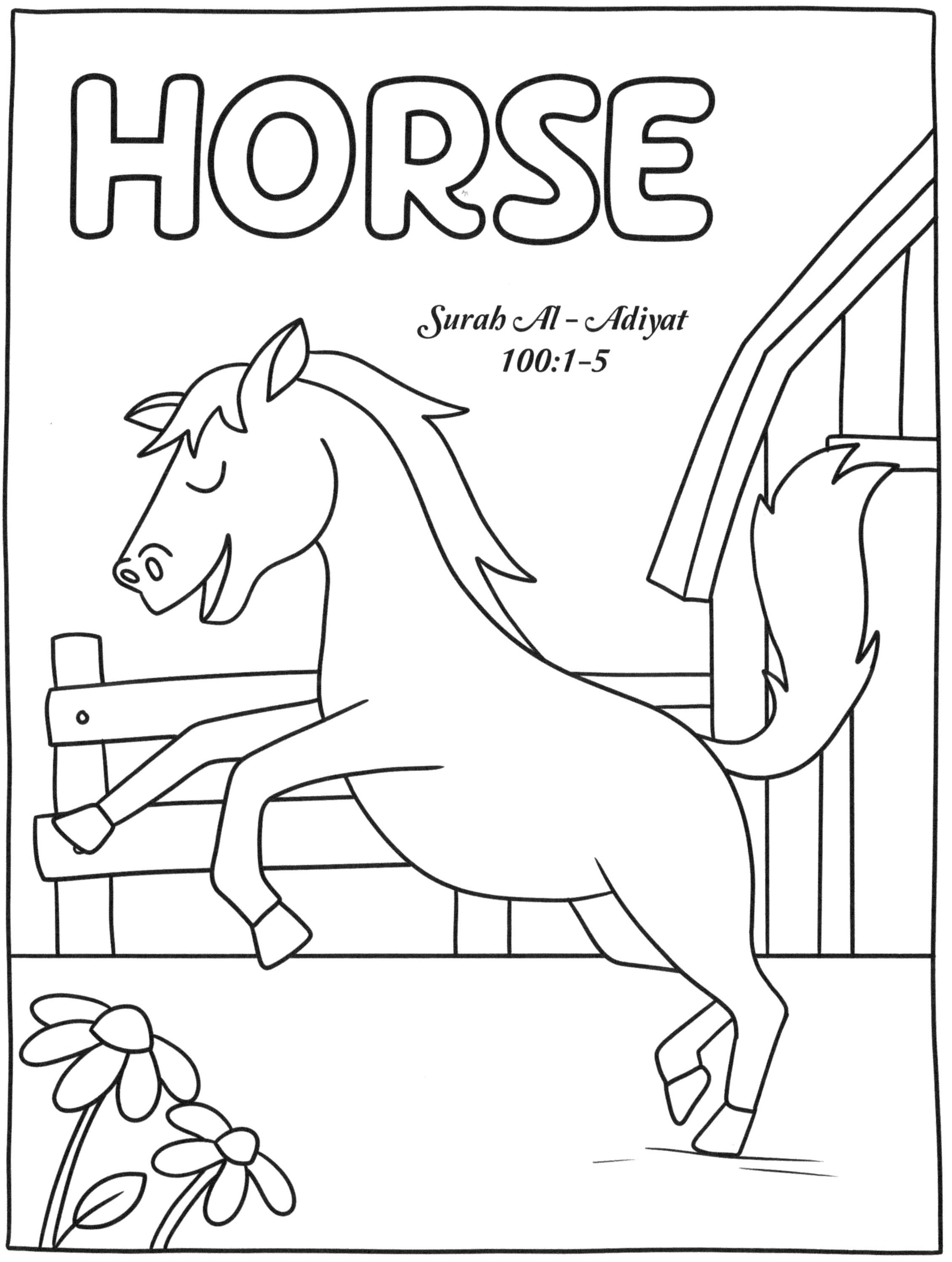
HORSE
Surah Al - Adiyat
100:1-5

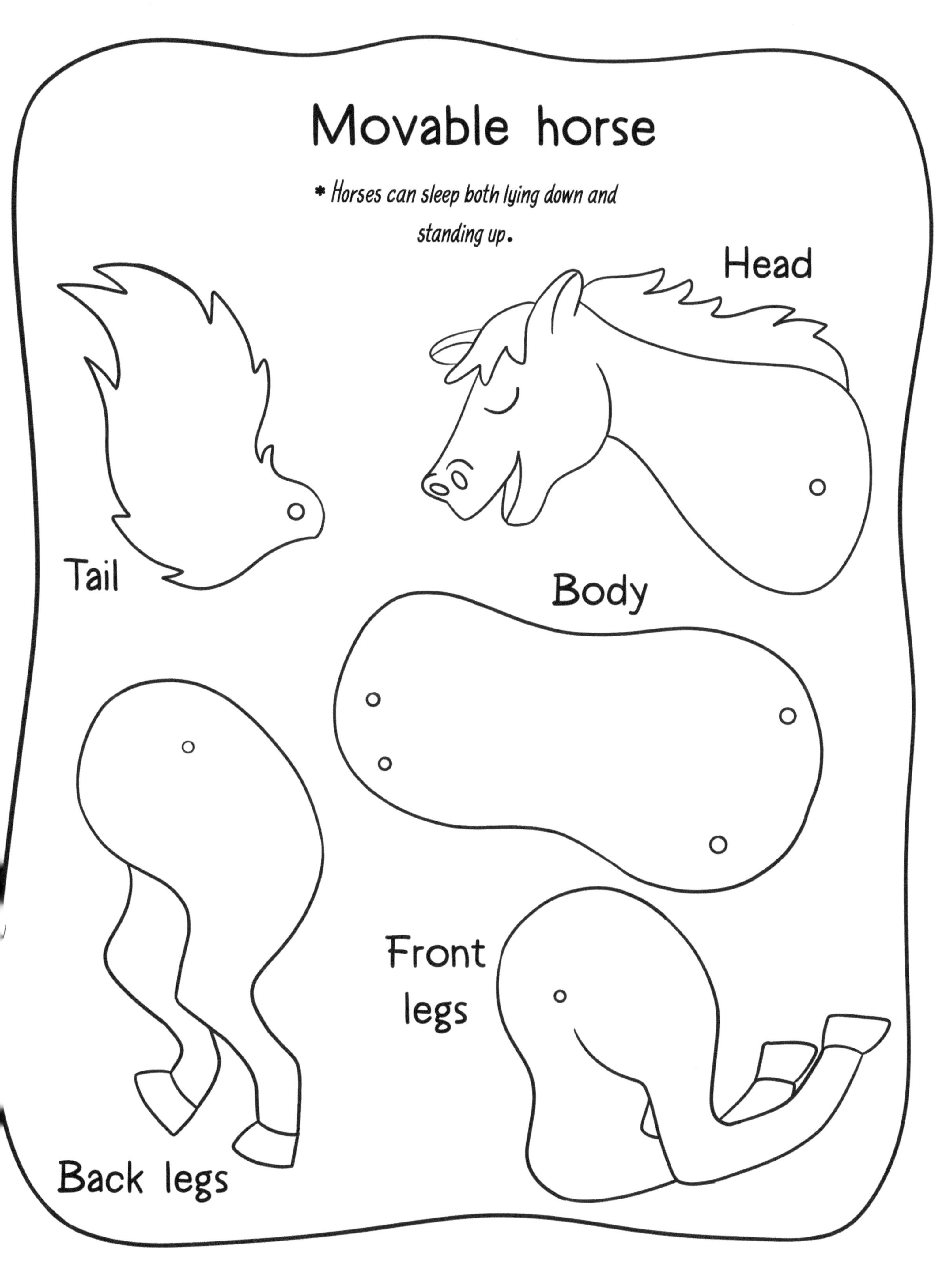
Movable horse
* Horses can sleep both lying down and standing up.
Head
Tail
Body
Front legs
Back legs

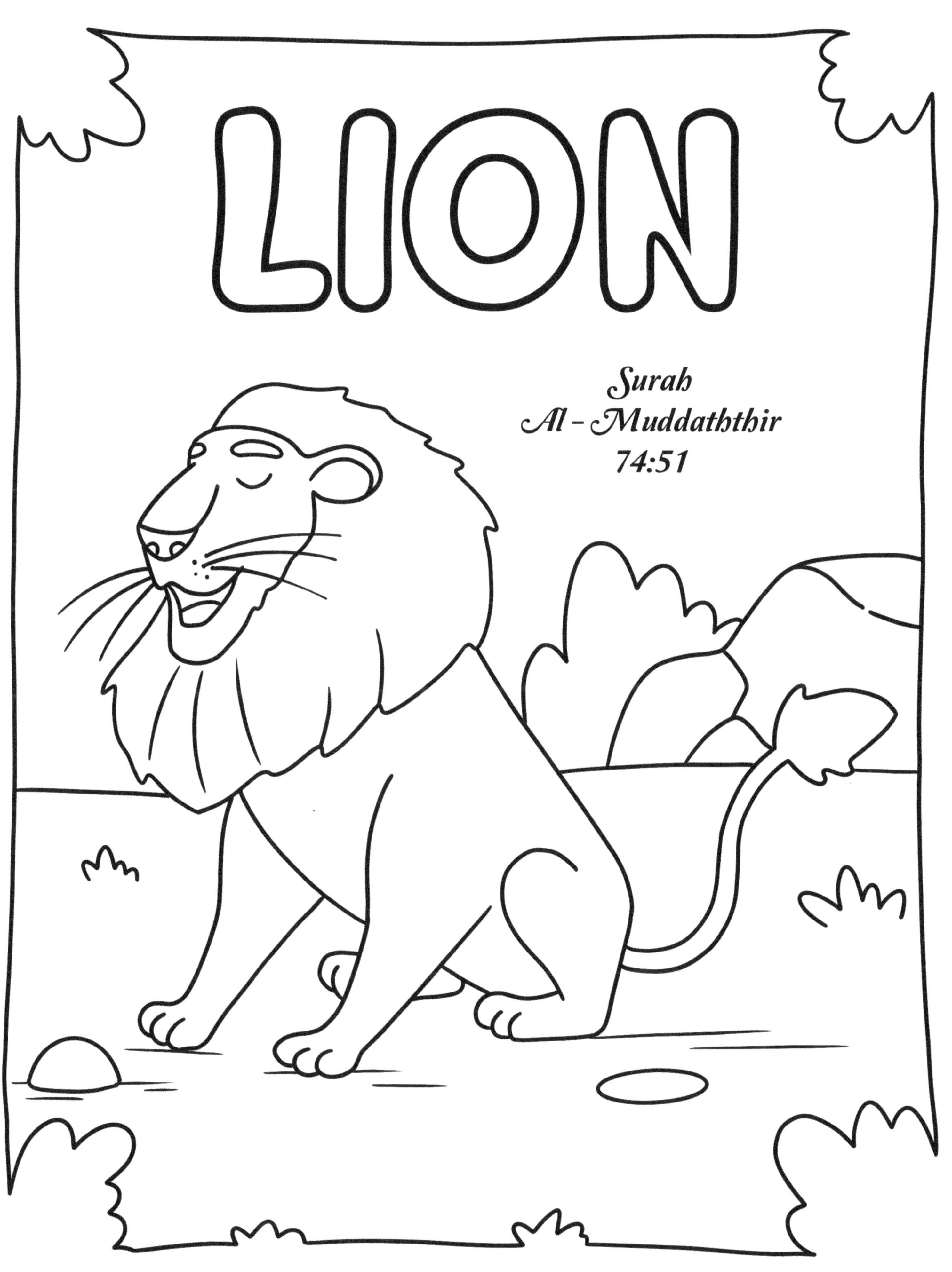
LION
Surah
Al - Muddaththir
74:51

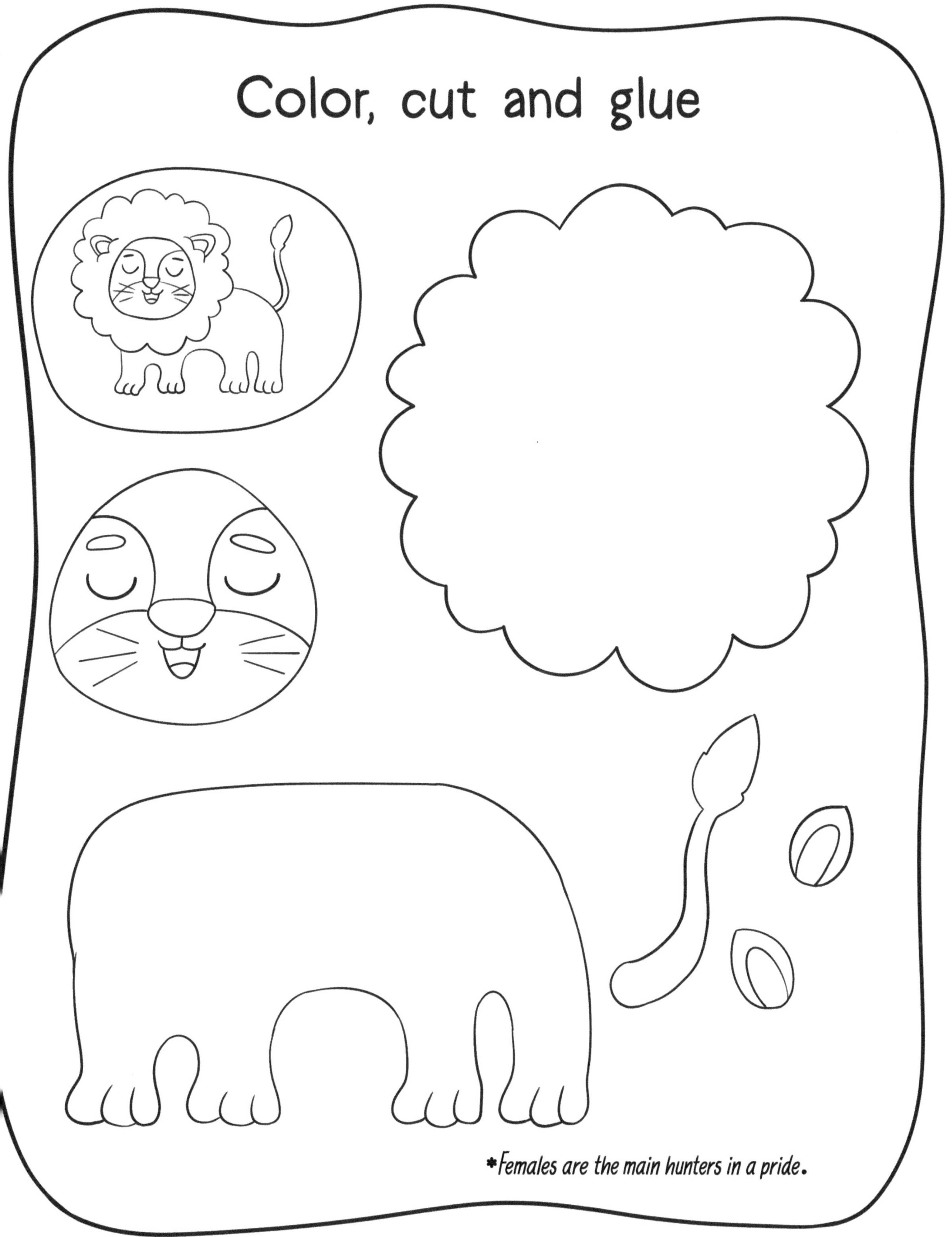
Color, cut and glue
*Females are the main hunters in a pride.

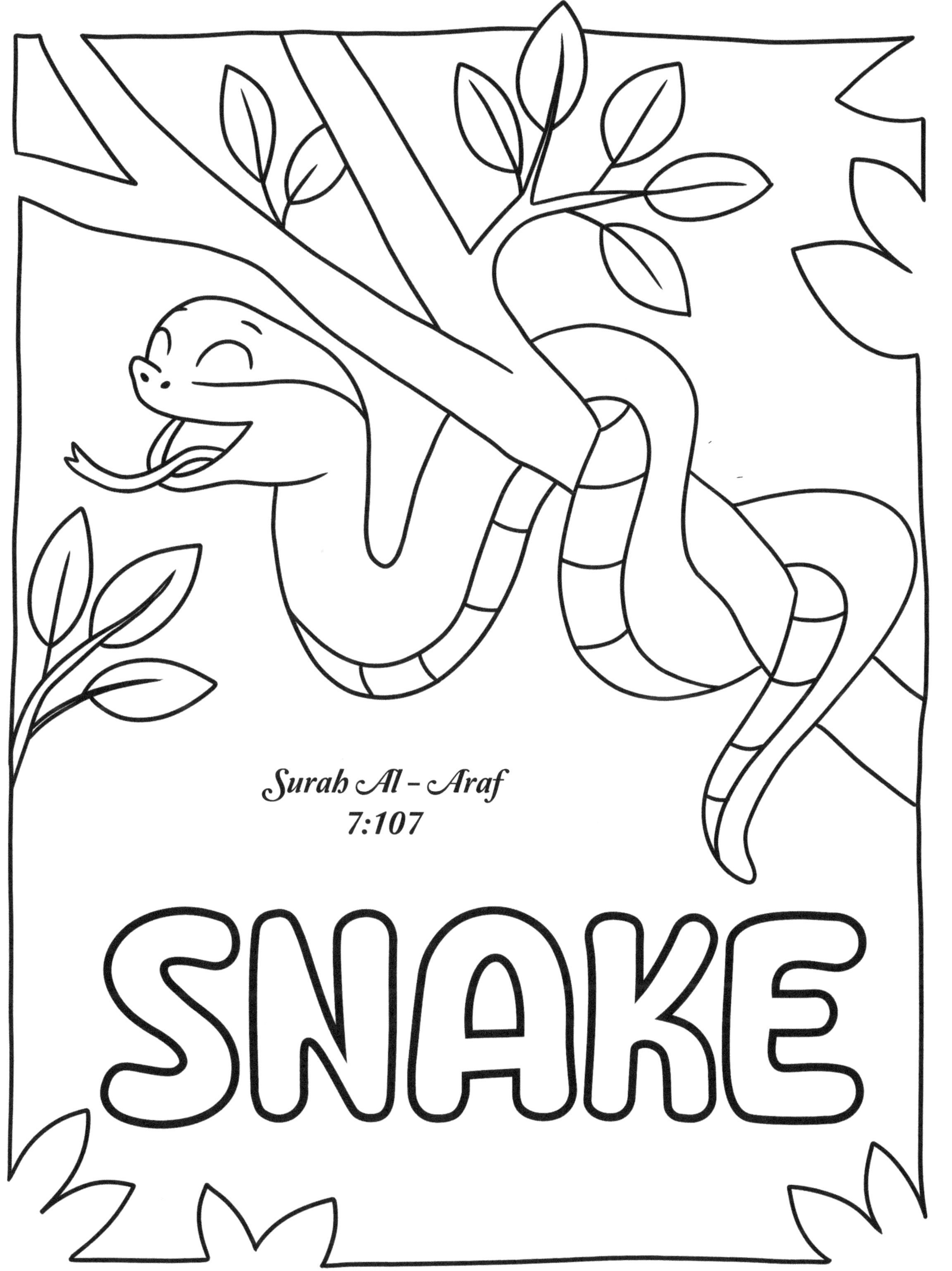
Surah Al - Araf
7:107
SNAKE

Word search

s d f t r g s n a k e f
c e a b n g o u c e m h
a x n m r a t t l e j i
l w g n x g p k z e c s
e c s s l i t h e r h s
s r u n d h i k g t n x

Fangs
Hiss
Snake
Slither
Scales
Rattle

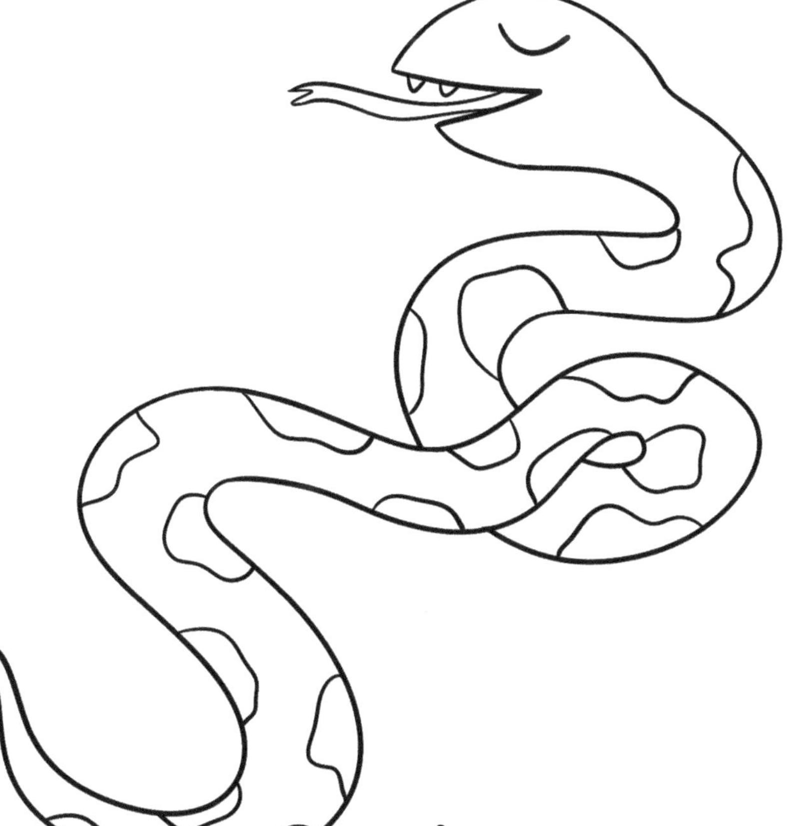

*A snakes tongue is used to smell .

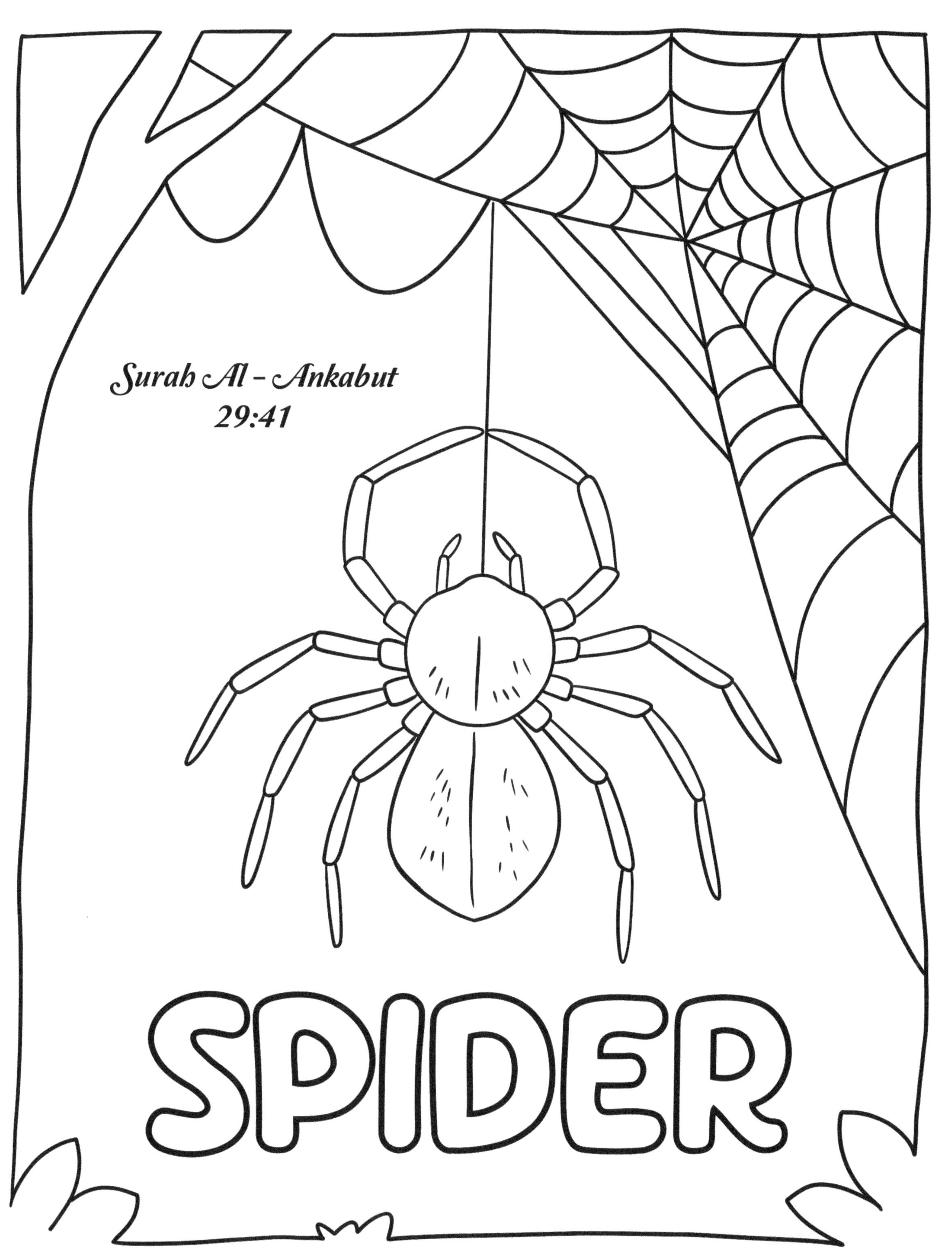
Surah Al - Ankabut
29:41
SPIDER

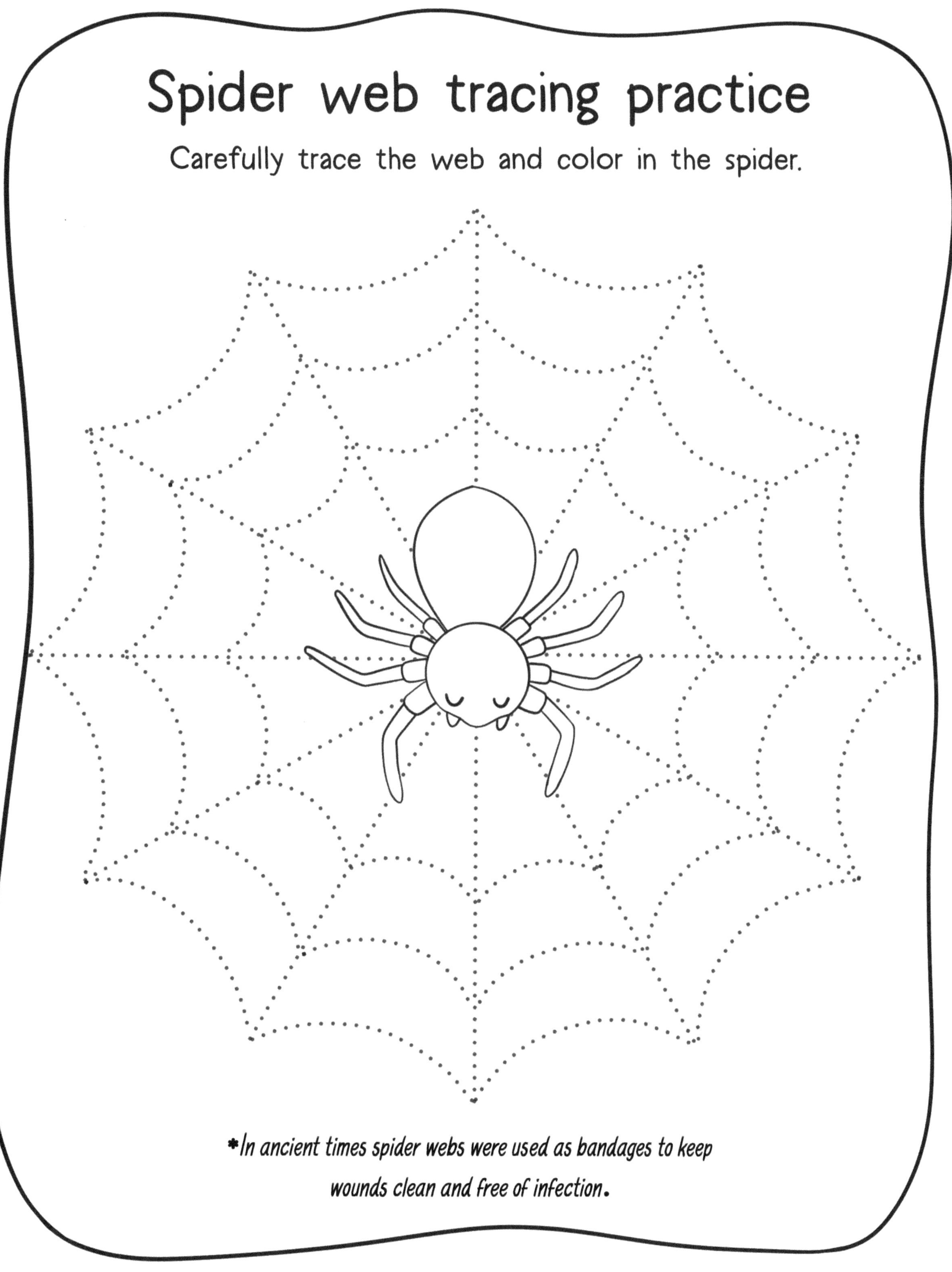
Spider web tracing practice
Carefully trace the web and color in the spider.
*In ancient times spider webs were used as bandages to keep wounds clean and free of infection.

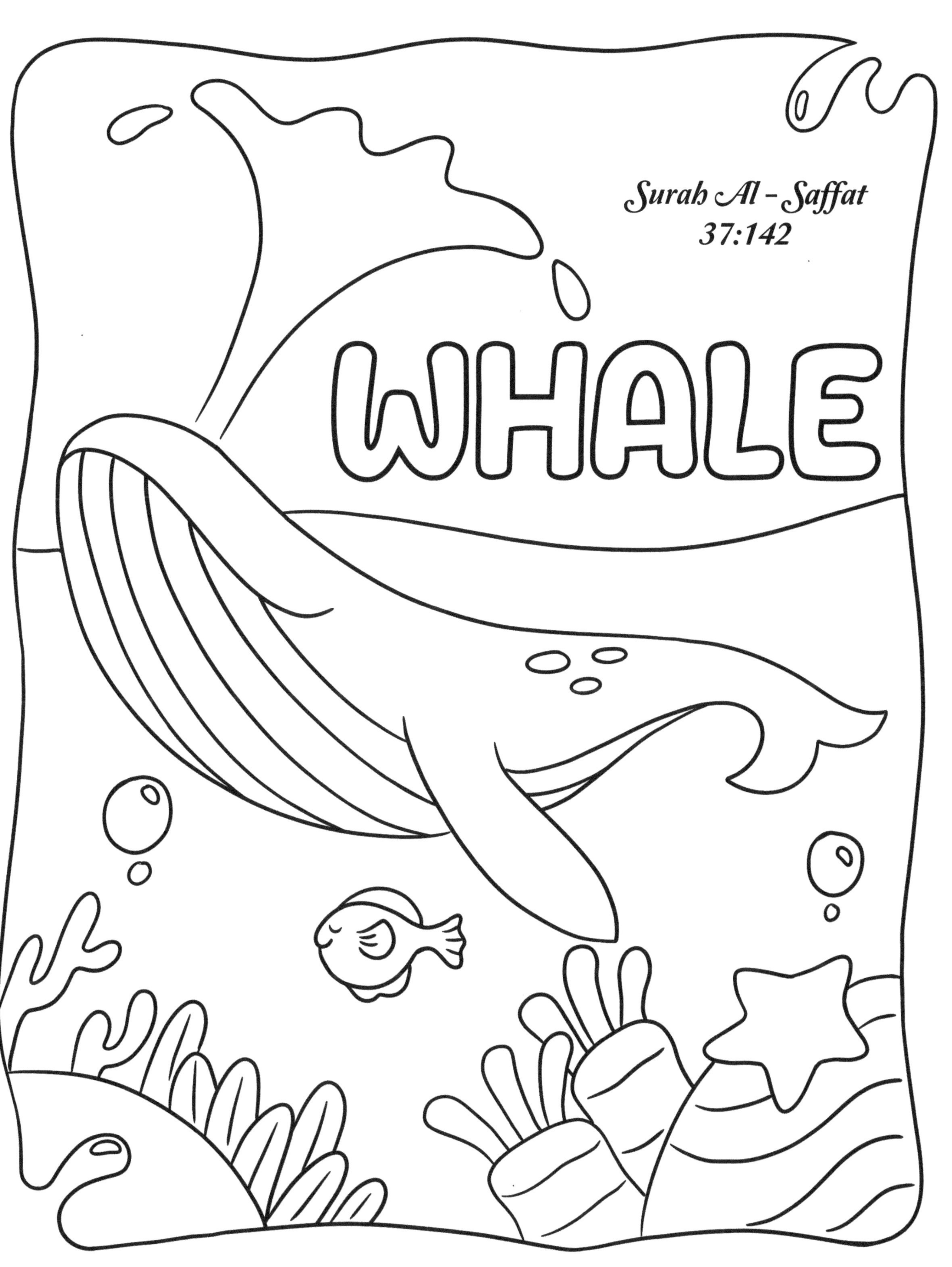
Surah Al - Saffat
37:142
WHALE

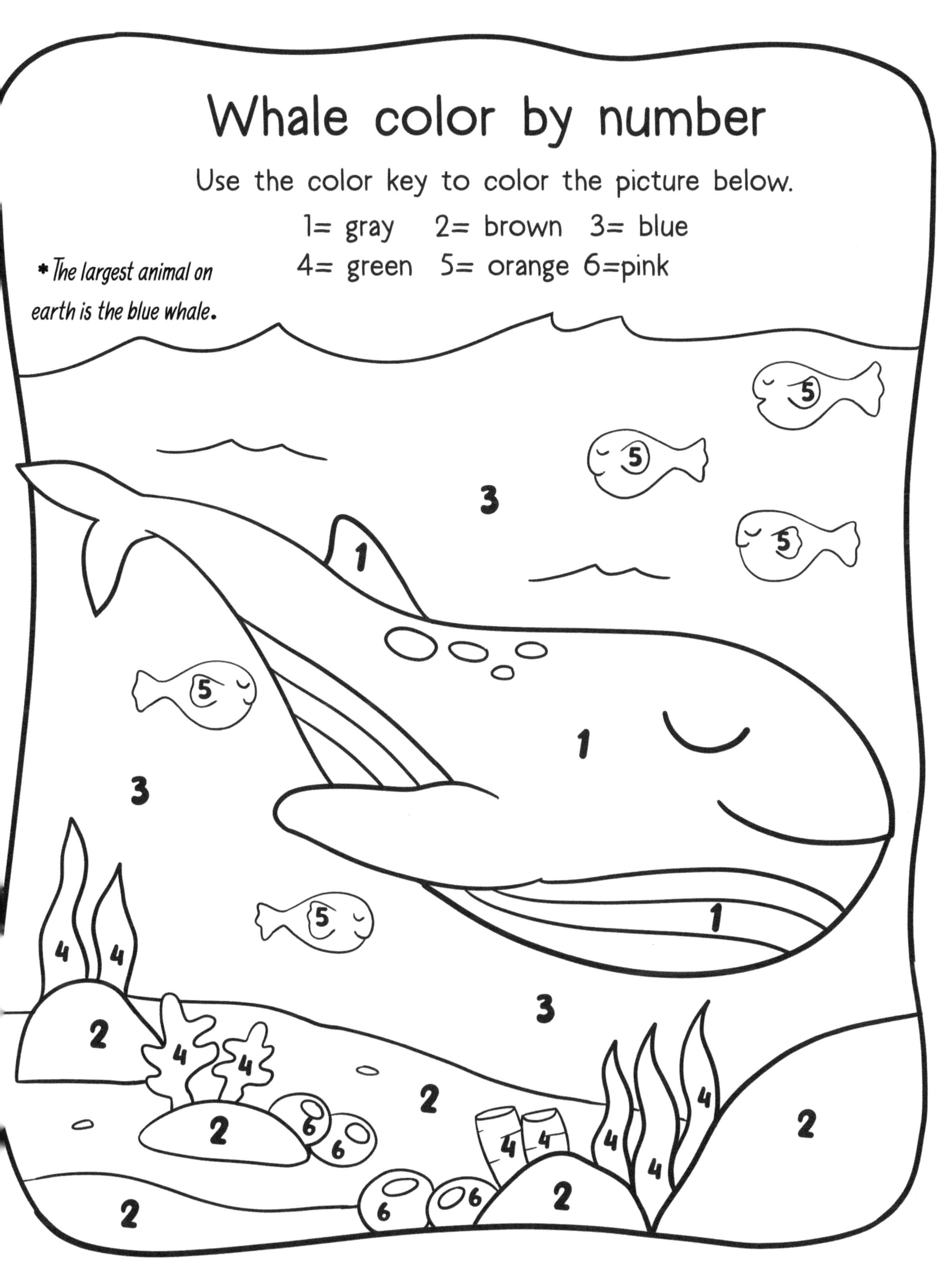
Whale color by number
Use the color key to color the picture below.
1= gray 2= brown 3= blue
4= green 5= orange 6=pink
* The largest animal on earth is the blue whale.
5
5
5
3
1
5
1
3
5
1
4
4
3
2
4
4
2
2
6
6
4
4
4
4
2
2
6
6
2

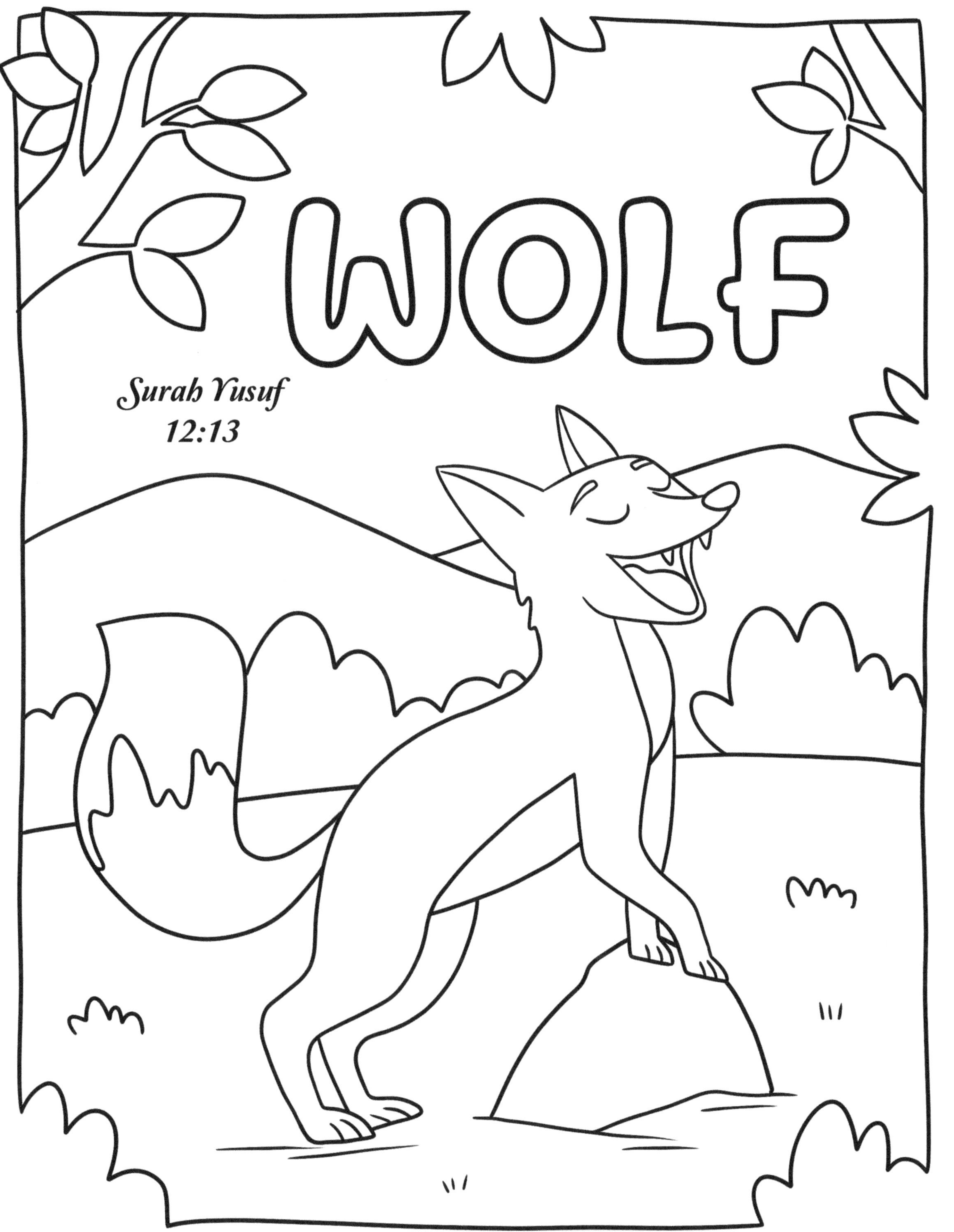
WOLF
Surah Yusuf
12:13

Word search

*A wolves howl can be heard up to 9 miles away.

r	d	f	t	r	g	p	t	a	k	m	h
b	e	s	b	n	g	o	u	c	e	m	o
h	x	t	m	o	o	n	a	p	d	j	w
u	w	v	n	x	g	p	k	z	e	c	l
o	c	z	g	u	i	k	l	z	n	h	l
v	r	u	n	d	h	i	k	g	t	n	x

Howl

Pack

Pup

Den

Hunter

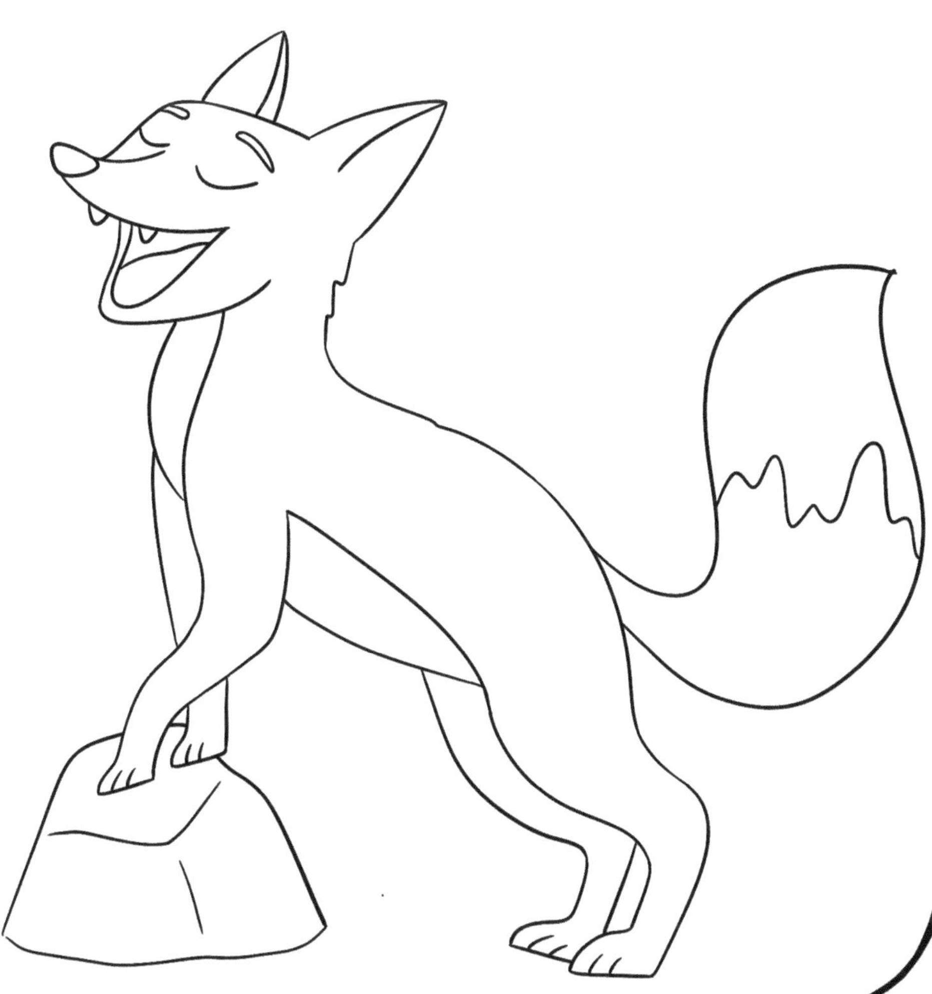

What is your favorite animal from the Quran?

Draw and explain!

www.ingramcontent.com/pod-product-compliance
Lightning Source LLC
LaVergne TN
LVHW060642110826
845147LV00018B/1024

9798989970377